Baseball Game Stats Book

Keep Your Own Records

(Simplified Version)

100 Games Edition

Team Colors series

Baseball Game Stats Book: Keep Your Own Records
(Simplified Version)
100 Games Edition

Copyright © 2016 by R.J. Foster and Richard B. Foster

All rights reserved.

No part of this book may be reproduced or transmitted in any form or by any means without written permission of the authors.

Keep Your Own Records series of books:

Copyright © 2016 by Richard B. Foster

All rights reserved.

No part of this series of books may be reproduced or transmitted in any form or by any means without written permission of the author.

Use this book for recording your baseball team's stats. Keep track of At-Bats (AB), Hits, Runs, Home Runs (HR), Runs Batted In (RBI), and Stolen Bases (SB). You can record up to 100 games with this book.

Game One

Player	AB	Hits	Runs	HR	RBI	SB
_____						
_____						
_____						
_____						
_____						
_____						
_____						
_____						
_____						
_____						
_____						
_____						
_____						
_____						
_____						
_____						
_____						

Game Two

Player	AB	Hits	Runs	HR	RBI	SB
_____						
_____						
_____						
_____						
_____						
_____						
_____						
_____						
_____						
_____						
_____						
_____						
_____						
_____						

Game Three

Player	AB	Hits	Runs	HR	RBI	SB
_____						
_____						
_____						
_____						
_____						
_____						
_____						
_____						
_____						
_____						
_____						
_____						
_____						
_____						
_____						
_____						

Game Four

Player	AB	Hits	Runs	HR	RBI	SB
_____						
_____						
_____						
_____						
_____						
_____						
_____						
_____						
_____						
_____						
_____						
_____						
_____						
_____						
_____						

Game Five

Player	AB	Hits	Runs	HR	RBI	SB
_____						
_____						
_____						
_____						
_____						
_____						
_____						
_____						
_____						
_____						
_____						
_____						
_____						
_____						
_____						
_____						
_____						
_____						
_____						

Game Six

Player	AB	Hits	Runs	HR	RBI	SB

Game Seven

Player	AB	Hits	Runs	HR	RBI	SB
_____						
_____						
_____						
_____						
_____						
_____						
_____						
_____						
_____						
_____						
_____						
_____						
_____						
_____						
_____						
_____						
_____						

Game Eight

Player	AB	Hits	Runs	HR	RBI	SB

Game Nine

Player	AB	Hits	Runs	HR	RBI	SB
_____						
_____						
_____						
_____						
_____						
_____						
_____						
_____						
_____						
_____						
_____						
_____						
_____						
_____						
_____						
_____						

Game Ten

Player	AB	Hits	Runs	HR	RBI	SB

Game Eleven

Player	AB	Hits	Runs	HR	RBI	SB

Game Twelve

Player	AB	Hits	Runs	HR	RBI	SB

Game Thirteen

Player	AB	Hits	Runs	HR	RBI	SB
_____						
_____						
_____						
_____						
_____						
_____						
_____						
_____						
_____						
_____						
_____						
_____						
_____						
_____						

Game Fourteen

Player	AB	Hits	Runs	HR	RBI	SB
_____						
_____						
_____						
_____						
_____						
_____						
_____						
_____						
_____						
_____						
_____						
_____						
_____						
_____						
_____						
_____						

Game Fifteen

Player	AB	Hits	Runs	HR	RBI	SB
_____						
_____						
_____						
_____						
_____						
_____						
_____						
_____						
_____						
_____						
_____						
_____						
_____						
_____						
_____						

Game Sixteen

Player	AB	Hits	Runs	HR	RBI	SB

Game Seventeen

Player	AB	Hits	Runs	HR	RBI	SB
_____						
_____						
_____						
_____						
_____						
_____						
_____						
_____						
_____						
_____						
_____						
_____						
_____						
_____						
_____						

Game Eighteen

Player	AB	Hits	Runs	HR	RBI	SB

Game Nineteen

Player	AB	Hits	Runs	HR	RBI	SB
_____						
_____						
_____						
_____						
_____						
_____						
_____						
_____						
_____						
_____						
_____						
_____						
_____						
_____						
_____						
_____						

Game Twenty

Player	AB	Hits	Runs	HR	RBI	SB
_____						
_____						
_____						
_____						
_____						
_____						
_____						
_____						
_____						
_____						
_____						
_____						
_____						
_____						
_____						
_____						

Game Twenty-One

Player	AB	Hits	Runs	HR	RBI	SB
_____						
_____						
_____						
_____						
_____						
_____						
_____						
_____						
_____						
_____						
_____						
_____						

Game Twenty-Two

Player	AB	Hits	Runs	HR	RBI	SB
_____						
_____						
_____						
_____						
_____						
_____						
_____						
_____						
_____						
_____						
_____						
_____						
_____						
_____						
_____						

Game Twenty-Three

Player	AB	Hits	Runs	HR	RBI	SB

Game Twenty-Four

Player	AB	Hits	Runs	HR	RBI	SB

Game Twenty-Five

Player	AB	Hits	Runs	HR	RBI	SB
_____						
_____						
_____						
_____						
_____						
_____						
_____						
_____						
_____						
_____						
_____						
_____						
_____						
_____						
_____						

Game Twenty-Six

Player	AB	Hits	Runs	HR	RBI	SB

Game Twenty-Seven

Player	AB	Hits	Runs	HR	RBI	SB
_____						
_____						
_____						
_____						
_____						
_____						
_____						
_____						
_____						
_____						
_____						
_____						
_____						
_____						

Game Twenty-Eight

Player	AB	Hits	Runs	HR	RBI	SB

Game Twenty-Nine

Player	AB	Hits	Runs	HR	RBI	SB

Game Thirty

Player	AB	Hits	Runs	HR	RBI	SB

Game Thirty-One

Player	AB	Hits	Runs	HR	RBI	SB

Game Thirty-Two

Player	AB	Hits	Runs	HR	RBI	SB
_____						
_____						
_____						
_____						
_____						
_____						
_____						
_____						
_____						
_____						
_____						
_____						
_____						
_____						
_____						
_____						

Game Thirty-Three

Player	AB	Hits	Runs	HR	RBI	SB
_____						
_____						
_____						
_____						
_____						
_____						
_____						
_____						
_____						
_____						
_____						
_____						
_____						
_____						

Game Thirty-Four

Player	AB	Hits	Runs	HR	RBI	SB
_____						
_____						
_____						
_____						
_____						
_____						
_____						
_____						
_____						
_____						
_____						
_____						
_____						
_____						
_____						
_____						

Game Thirty-Five

Player	AB	Hits	Runs	HR	RBI	SB
_____						
_____						
_____						
_____						
_____						
_____						
_____						
_____						
_____						
_____						
_____						
_____						
_____						
_____						
_____						
_____						
_____						

Game Thirty-Six

Player	AB	Hits	Runs	HR	RBI	SB
_____						
_____						
_____						
_____						
_____						
_____						
_____						
_____						
_____						
_____						
_____						
_____						
_____						
_____						
_____						

Game Thirty-Seven

Player	AB	Hits	Runs	HR	RBI	SB

Game Thirty-Eight

Player	AB	Hits	Runs	HR	RBI	SB

Game Thirty-Nine

Player	AB	Hits	Runs	HR	RBI	SB

Game Forty

Player	AB	Hits	Runs	HR	RBI	SB

Game Forty-One

Player	AB	Hits	Runs	HR	RBI	SB

Game Forty-Two

Player	AB	Hits	Runs	HR	RBI	SB
_____						
_____						
_____						
_____						
_____						
_____						
_____						
_____						
_____						
_____						
_____						
_____						
_____						
_____						

Game Forty-Three

Player	AB	Hits	Runs	HR	RBI	SB
_____						
_____						
_____						
_____						
_____						
_____						
_____						
_____						
_____						
_____						
_____						
_____						
_____						
_____						

Game Forty-Four

Player	AB	Hits	Runs	HR	RBI	SB
_____						
_____						
_____						
_____						
_____						
_____						
_____						
_____						
_____						
_____						
_____						
_____						
_____						
_____						

Game Forty-Five

Player	AB	Hits	Runs	HR	RBI	SB

Game Forty-Six

Player	AB	Hits	Runs	HR	RBI	SB
_____						
_____						
_____						
_____						
_____						
_____						
_____						
_____						
_____						
_____						
_____						
_____						
_____						
_____						
_____						

Game Forty-Seven

Player	AB	Hits	Runs	HR	RBI	SB

Game Forty-Eight

Player	AB	Hits	Runs	HR	RBI	SB

Game Forty-Nine

Player	AB	Hits	Runs	HR	RBI	SB

Game Fifty

Player	AB	Hits	Runs	HR	RBI	SB
_____						
_____						
_____						
_____						
_____						
_____						
_____						
_____						
_____						
_____						
_____						
_____						
_____						
_____						

Game Fifty-One

Player	AB	Hits	Runs	HR	RBI	SB
_____						
_____						
_____						
_____						
_____						
_____						
_____						
_____						
_____						
_____						
_____						
_____						
_____						
_____						
_____						
_____						

Game Fifty-Two

Player	AB	Hits	Runs	HR	RBI	SB
_____						
_____						
_____						
_____						
_____						
_____						
_____						
_____						
_____						
_____						
_____						
_____						
_____						
_____						

Game Fifty-Three

Player	AB	Hits	Runs	HR	RBI	SB

Game Fifty-Four

Player	AB	Hits	Runs	HR	RBI	SB

Game Fifty-Five

Player	AB	Hits	Runs	HR	RBI	SB

Game Fifty-Six

Player	AB	Hits	Runs	HR	RBI	SB

Game Fifty-Seven

Player	AB	Hits	Runs	HR	RBI	SB

Game Fifty-Eight

Player	AB	Hits	Runs	HR	RBI	SB

Game Fifty-Nine

Player	AB	Hits	Runs	HR	RBI	SB

Game Sixty

Player	AB	Hits	Runs	HR	RBI	SB
_____						
_____						
_____						
_____						
_____						
_____						
_____						
_____						
_____						
_____						
_____						
_____						
_____						
_____						
_____						

Game Sixty-One

Player	AB	Hits	Runs	HR	RBI	SB

Game Sixty-Two

Player	AB	Hits	Runs	HR	RBI	SB

Game Sixty-Three

Player	AB	Hits	Runs	HR	RBI	SB

Game Sixty-Four

Player	AB	Hits	Runs	HR	RBI	SB

Game Sixty-Five

Player	AB	Hits	Runs	HR	RBI	SB
_____						
_____						
_____						
_____						
_____						
_____						
_____						
_____						
_____						
_____						
_____						
_____						
_____						

Game Sixty-Six

Player	AB	Hits	Runs	HR	RBI	SB

Game Sixty-Seven

Player	AB	Hits	Runs	HR	RBI	SB

Game Sixty-Eight

Player	AB	Hits	Runs	HR	RBI	SB
_____						
_____						
_____						
_____						
_____						
_____						
_____						
_____						
_____						
_____						
_____						
_____						
_____						
_____						
_____						
_____						
_____						

Game Sixty-Nine

Player	AB	Hits	Runs	HR	RBI	SB

Game Seventy

Player	AB	Hits	Runs	HR	RBI	SB

Game Seventy-One

Player	AB	Hits	Runs	HR	RBI	SB

Game Seventy-Two

Player	AB	Hits	Runs	HR	RBI	SB
_____						
_____						
_____						
_____						
_____						
_____						
_____						
_____						
_____						
_____						
_____						
_____						
_____						
_____						
_____						

Game Seventy-Three

Player	AB	Hits	Runs	HR	RBI	SB

Game Seventy-Four

Player	AB	Hits	Runs	HR	RBI	SB

Game Seventy-Five

Player	AB	Hits	Runs	HR	RBI	SB

Game Seventy-Six

Player	AB	Hits	Runs	HR	RBI	SB

Game Seventy-Seven

Player	AB	Hits	Runs	HR	RBI	SB

Game Seventy-Eight

Player	AB	Hits	Runs	HR	RBI	SB

Game Seventy-Nine

Player	AB	Hits	Runs	HR	RBI	SB
_____						
_____						
_____						
_____						
_____						
_____						
_____						
_____						
_____						
_____						
_____						
_____						
_____						
_____						

Game Eighty

Player	AB	Hits	Runs	HR	RBI	SB

Game Eighty-One

Player	AB	Hits	Runs	HR	RBI	SB
_____						
_____						
_____						
_____						
_____						
_____						
_____						
_____						
_____						
_____						
_____						
_____						
_____						
_____						
_____						
_____						

Game Eighty-Two

Player	AB	Hits	Runs	HR	RBI	SB
_____						
_____						
_____						
_____						
_____						
_____						
_____						
_____						
_____						
_____						
_____						
_____						
_____						

Game Eighty-Three

Player	AB	Hits	Runs	HR	RBI	SB

Game Eighty-Four

Player	AB	Hits	Runs	HR	RBI	SB

Game Eighty-Five

Player	AB	Hits	Runs	HR	RBI	SB
_____						
_____						
_____						
_____						
_____						
_____						
_____						
_____						
_____						
_____						
_____						
_____						

Game Eighty-Six

Player	AB	Hits	Runs	HR	RBI	SB

Game Eighty-Seven

Player	AB	Hits	Runs	HR	RBI	SB

Game Eighty-Eight

Player	AB	Hits	Runs	HR	RBI	SB
_____						
_____						
_____						
_____						
_____						
_____						
_____						
_____						
_____						
_____						
_____						
_____						
_____						
_____						

Game Eighty-Nine

Player	AB	Hits	Runs	HR	RBI	SB
_____						
_____						
_____						
_____						
_____						
_____						
_____						
_____						
_____						
_____						
_____						
_____						

Game Ninety

Player	AB	Hits	Runs	HR	RBI	SB

Game Ninety-One

Player	AB	Hits	Runs	HR	RBI	SB

Game Ninety-Two

Player	AB	Hits	Runs	HR	RBI	SB

Game Ninety-Three

Player	AB	Hits	Runs	HR	RBI	SB

Game Ninety-Four

Player	AB	Hits	Runs	HR	RBI	SB

Game Ninety-Five

Player	AB	Hits	Runs	HR	RBI	SB

Game Ninety-Six

Player	AB	Hits	Runs	HR	RBI	SB

Game Ninety-Seven

Player	AB	Hits	Runs	HR	RBI	SB

Game Ninety-Eight

Player	AB	Hits	Runs	HR	RBI	SB

Game Ninety-Nine

Player	AB	Hits	Runs	HR	RBI	SB

Game One Hundred

Player	AB	Hits	Runs	HR	RBI	SB
_____						
_____						
_____						
_____						
_____						
_____						
_____						
_____						
_____						
_____						
_____						
_____						
_____						
_____						
_____						

Made in the USA
Middletown, DE
08 May 2019